365 Days of Horses: Inspirational Quotes For the Horse Lover

Foreword by M.G. Keefe

365 Days of Horses:

Inspirational Quotes for the Horse Lover

Hot Tropica Books Publication

February 2013

Copyright © 2013 Foreword by M.G. Keefe

Cover illustration copyright © Jackson Falls

ISBN 10: 1482357011
ISBN 13: 978-1482357011

Published by: **Hot Tropica Books**

265 Days of Horses

Blurb:

There is no creature more majestic, and more fascinating than a horse. Horses have been used around the world for thousands of years. Even when technology has replaced the horse for the most part, we still judge an engine's power in horsepower.

This collection of memorable quotes is meant to inspire and amuse the horse lover in all of us. Start the day off with a smile by reading a horse quote every day of the year or just read the book in one sitting.

This book also makes a terrific gift for the horse lover.

If you want a stable friendship, get a horse. ~ Unknown

Foreword by MG Keefe

The horse is an amazingly powerful and majestic beast. I still see it as a small miracle every time I get on the back of a horse and it listens to me.

The horse is docile and submissive. The horse is ten times my size, weighs nearly a thousand pounds and I am a little over a hundred, yet the horse takes care of its rider. Just as man takes care of his horses needs, the horse takes care of man. He would give his life, and take orders to march into the heat of battle, or go over a jump, not knowing what lies on the other side.

The horse has a long history at man's side. We tamed the wild horse and used his strength and power to help us. We learned to ride them, and pull wagons, even plowing the fields. The horses didn't have to be paid in gold, they just need food and shelter.

It's been a wonderful partnership.

Until the last couple hundred years we have seen the need for horses. Lately they have been replaced more and more by modern technology. But even our cars are judged in power and strength by horsepower.

Horses have set the standard.

But even when we don't need them for everyday life, horses will always have a special place in our lives. Love comes in many forms, shapes, and sizes, but the best loves come horse shaped.

365 Days of Horses

Day 1: Animals do not admire each other. A horse does not admire its companion. ~ Thomas Mann

Day 2: There's nothing so good for the inside of a man as the outside of a horse. ~ Ronald Reagan

Day 3: A bad day of riding is better than a good day of fishing. ~ Unknown

Day 4: A dog looks up to a man, a cat looks down, but a horse looks him in the eye and sees him as an equal. ~ Unknown

Day 5: A dog may be man's best friend, but the horse wrote history. ~ Unknown

Day 6: A fly, sir, may sting a stately horse, and make him wince, but one is but an insect, and the other is a horse still. ~ Samuel Johnson

Day 7: A good rider can hear his horse speak to him, a great rider can hear his horse whisper, but a bad rider won't hear his horse even if it screams at him. ~ Unknown

Day 8: A horse doesn't care how much you don't know until he knows how much you care. ~ Pat Parelli

Day 9: A horse is an angel without wings. ~ Unknown

Day 10: A horse is like a best friend. They are always there to nuzzle you and make your life a better place. ~ Unknown

Day 11: A horse is like a violin. First it must be tuned, and when tuned, it must be accurately played. ~

Day 12: A polo pony is like a motorbike with a mind of its own, weighing half a ton. ~ Unknown

Day 13: Passion is passion. It's the excitement between the tedious spaces, and it doesn't matter where it's directed...It can be coins or sports or politics or horses or music or faith...the saddest people I've ever met in life are the ones who don't care deeply about anything at all. ~ Nicholas Sparks

Day 14: "God alert!" Blackjack yelled. "It's the wine dude!" Mr. D sighed in exasperation. "The next person, or horse who calls me the wine dude will end up in a bottle of Merlot!" ~ Rick Riordan

Day 15: If I had a dime for every time I thought of a horse's beauty, I'd have enough to buy one. ~ Unknown

Day 16: A horse never runs so fast as when he has other horses to catch up and outpace. ~ Ovid

Day 17: And if I were president, I'd go out there and I'd emphasize the things I have done and I'd say, "Some things haven't worked, and I'm sorry about that, but I keep trying." And I'm—and I think the president is a very viable candidate, and you are going to have a real horse race no matter who the Republican nominee is. ~ Michael Bloomberg

Day 18: Marry me and I'll never look at another horse. ~ Groucho Marx

Day 19: If time were the wicked sheriff in a horse opera, I'd pay for riding lessons and take his gun away. ~ W.H. Auden

Day 20: If the horse does not enjoy his work, his rider will have no joy. ~ H.H. Isenbart

Day 21: If a horse has four legs and I'm riding it, I think I can win. ~ Charles Caleb Colton

Day 22: It's hard to lead a cavalry charge if you think you look funny on a horse. ~ Adlai E. Stevenson

Day 23: The only time some people work like a horse is when the boss rides them. ~ Gabriel Heatter

Day 24: Vampires are sexy to a woman perhaps because the fantasy is similar to that of a man on a white horse sweeping her off to paradise. ~ Frank Langella

Day 25: If you want a stable friendship, get a horse. ~ Unknown

Day 26: There is a touch of divinity even in brutes, and a special halo about a horse, that should forever exempt him from indignities. ~ Herman Melville

Day 27: I played a great horse yesterday! It took seven horses to beat him. ~ Henny Youngman

Day 28: I split my time between Santa Barbara and Aspen. I live on a pretty fast horse. ~ Kevin Costner

Day 29: Animals do not admire each other. A horse does not admire its companion. ~ Thomas Mann

Day 30: It excited me no matter how much machinery replaces the horse, the work it can do is still measured in horsepower…even in this space age. And although a riding horse often weighs half a ton, and a big drafter a full ton, either can be led about by a piece of string if he has been wisely trained. This to me is a constant source of wonder and challenge. ~ Marguret Henry

Day 31: Don't worry about the horse being blind. Just load the wagon. ~ John Madden

Day 32: A good horse is not apt to jump over a bank, if left to guide himself, I let mine pick his own way. ~ Buffalo Bill

Day 33: I'd sit on a horse and forget I was even sick. ~ Anne Romney

Day 34: Religion needs a baptism of horse sense. ~ Billy Sunday

Day 35: Life is short. Hug your horse. ~ Unknown

Day 36: If you spend all day on horseback, and you hop off, you walk around like you still have a horse beneath your legs. And it affects your shoulders. They fall. ~ Heath Ledger

Day 37: When my horse is running good, I don't stop to give him sugar. ~ Douglas Horton

Day 38: My mom never taught me to wait for some prince on a white horse to sweep me off my feet. ~ Tyra Banks

Day 39: Few girls are as well shaped as a good horse. ~ Hannah Arendt

Day 40: Love means attention, which means looking after the things we love. We call this stable management. ~ George H. Morris

Day 41: I wouldn't mind starting to ride some more if I had a really good horse to just work a little bit with every day. ~ Robert Duvall

Day 42: The horse was so slow, the jockey kept a diary of the trip. ~ Henny Youngman

Day 43: A husband is very much like a house or a horse. ~ Anthony Trollope

Day 44: I think it was much better when you got on your horse and rode two miles to talk to your neighbor. ~ Laura Schlessinger

Day 45: My husband says if I spend one more weekend at a horse-show, he'll leave me. Darn, I'll miss him! ~

Day 46: I had daydreams and fantasies when I was growing up. I always wanted to live in a log cabin at the foot of a mountain. I would ride my horse to town and pick up my provisions. Then return to the cabin, with a big open fire, a record player and peace. ~ Linda McCartney

Day 47: Yes, I think that when the Bible refers to a horse or a horseman, that's exactly what it means. ~ Tim LaHaye

Day 48: There aren't a lot of guys like me left. But I'm a warhorse. I've been through it all. And you know something about warhorses? Through the sleet, through the snow, they just keep going. ~ Joel Silver

Day 49: Why, I'd horse whip you if I had a horse. ~ Groucho Marx

Day 50: My new horse was sold to me as a real gentleman to ride. He is. When we have to go over a fence, he insists on "Ladies first!" ~ Unknown

Day 51: Some people regard private enterprise as a predatory tiger to be shot. Others look on it as a cow they can milk. Not enough people see it as a healthy horse, pulling a sturdy wagon. ~ Sir Winston Churchill

Day 52: I would travel only by horse, given the choice. ~ Linda McCartney

Day 53: A canter is a cure for every evil. ~ Benjamin Disraeli

Day 54: Never approach a bull from the front, a horse from the rear, or a fool from any direction. ~ Cowboy saying

Day 55: I speak Spanish to God, Italian to women, French to men, and German to my horse. ~ Charles V

Day 56: The horse knows how to be a horse if we will leave him alone…but the riders don't know how to ride. What we should be doing is creating riders and that takes care of the horse immediately. ~ Charles De Kunffy

Day 57: There is something about riding down a street on a prancing horse that makes you feel like something, even when you ain't a thing. ~ Will Rogers

Day 58: A good horse makes short miles. ~ George Elliot

Day 59: Gypsy gold does not chink and glitter. It gleams in the sun and neighs in the dark. ~ Saying of the Gladdagh Gypsies of Galway

Day 60: A difference of opinion is what makes horse racing and missionaries. ~ Will Rogers

Day 61:The horse is a mirror to your soul…and sometimes you might not like what you see in a mirror. ~ Buck Brannaman

Day 62: Horses make a landscape look beautiful. ~ Alice Walker

Day 63: You don't break these animals, you come to an understanding with them. ~ Phil West

Day 64: All horses at least once deserve to be loved by a little girl. ~ Unknown

Day 65: A man in passion rides a horse that runs away with him. ~ Thomas Fuller

Day 66: Blame it or praise it, there's no denying the wild horse in us. ~ Virginia Woolfe

Day 67: Fierce as the fire and fleet as the wind. ~ A.L. Gordon

Day 68: Wild horses run unbridled or the spirit dies. ~ Unknown

Day 69: Keep calm and trot on. ~ Unknown

Day 70: Every horse thinks its own pack heaviest. ~Thomas Fuller

Day 71: A horse does not greet the sun and say, "Today will be better." It can only reflect upon days of past experiences. It is our job to create a positive past. ~ Karen West

Day 72: When I am an old horsewoman
        I shall wear turquoise and diamonds
        And a straw hat that doesn't suit me
        And I shall spend my social security on
        White wine and carrots
        And sit in my alleyway of my barn
        And listen to my horses breathe.
          ~ Patty Barnhart

Day 73: A horse is a thing of beauty…none will tire of looking at him as long as he displays himself in his splendor. ~ Unknown

Day 74: Horses are not lazy and they're not greedy and they're not spiteful, they're not hateful. They're not that way. But the human can sometimes only describe a horse in the way they view other human beings. ~ Buck Brannaman

Day 75: A good horse should seldom be spurred. ~Thomas Fuller

Day 76: There's nothing in life that's worth doing if it can't be done from the back of a horse. ~ Unknown

Day 77: A lovely horse is always an experience…It is an emotional experience that is spoiled by words. ~ Beryl Markham

Day 78: Whoever said diamonds are girl's best friend, clearly did not own a horse. ~ Unknown

Day 79: You can't tame a cowgirl. ~ Unknown

Day 80: Defoe says that there were a hundred thousand country fellows in his time ready to fight to the death against popery, without knowing whether popery was a man or a horse. ~ William Hazlitt

Day 81: Give a horse what he needs and he will give you his heart in return. ~ Unknown

Day 82: The horse knows. He knows if you know. He also knows if you don't know. ~ Ray Hunt

Day 83: The history of the west was written by a horse. ~ Unknown

Day 84: Riding this way is like playing a finely tuned instrument, at times delicate, at other times powerful…The true artist can play with equal dexterity a soft ballad or a crashing march. ~ Sally Swift

Day 85: If an ass goes travelling, he will not come a horse. ~ Thomas Fuller

Day 86: Sometimes even a cowboy has gotta swallow his pride to hold onto someone he loves. ~ Unknown

Day 87: Horses are incredibly forgiving. They fill in places we are not capable of filling in ourselves. ~ Buck Brannaman

Day 88: Show me your horses and I will tell you what you are. ~ English Proverb

Day 89: It ain't the clothes that make the cowgirl, it's the attitude and heart. ~ Unknown

Day 90: Take care to sell your horse before he dies. The art of life is passing losses on. ~ Robert Frost

Day 91: No hour o life is wasted that is spent in the saddle. ~ Sir Winston Churchill

Day 92: Horses and life, it's all the same to me. ~ Buck Brannaman

Day 93: A horse is poetry in motion. ~ Unknown

Day 94: A horse is the projection of peoples' dreams about themselves—strong, powerful, beautiful and it has the capability of giving us escape from our mundane existence. ~ Pam Brown

Day 95: Will is to grace as the horse is to the rider. ~ Saint Augustine

Day 96: Amazing horses. Truest majestic beauty. Running wild and free.~ Jessie Host

Day 97: The essential joy of being with horses is that it brings us in contact with the rare elements of grace, beauty, spirit, and fire. ~ Sharon Ralls Lemon

Day 98:Boots, chaps, and cowboy hats. Nothing else matters. ~ Unknown

Day 99: Where the leather is scarred there is a great story to tell. ~ Jimmy Tart

Day 100: I sit astride life like a bad rider on a horse. I only owe it to the horse's good nature that I am not thrown off at this very moment. ~ Ludwig Wittgenstein

Day 101: The profession of book writing makes horse racing look like a solid, stable business. ~ John Steinbeck

Day 102: Whenever I was upset by something in the papers, Jack always told me to be more tolerant, like a horse flicking away flies in the summer. ~ Jackie Kennedy

Day 103: It takes a good deal of physical courage to ride a horse. This, however, I have. I get it at about forty cents a flask, and take it as required. ~ Stephen Leacock

Day 104: I love watching a good horse do what he's bred to do—I guess that's what I like most about it. And I love to see good athletes do what they're bred to do. ~ Wilford Brimley

Day 105: Get off your horse and drink your milk. ~ John Wayne

Day 106: All music is folk music. I ain't never heard a horse sing a song. ~ Louis Armstrong

Day 107: What I used to do between my writing fits was feed my kids, ride my horse and go shopping for dog and cat food. ~ Anne McCaffrey

Day 108: People come and go but horses leave hoof prints on your heart. ~ Unknown

Day 109: We tolerate shapes in human beings that would horrify us if we saw them in a horse.~ Dean Inge

Day 110: The spirited horse, which will try to win the race of its own accord, will run even faster if encouraged. ~ Ovid

Day 111: When people say it's JUST a horse, they JUST don't understand. ~ Unknown

Day 112: A life without horses is taking a breath without air. ~ Unknown

Day 113: If I had a horse, I'd ride off in the sunset, where dreams, and shadows lie. To a life where pain and sorrow don't exist, and to where hopes and dreams become reality. ~ Unknown

Day 114: Ask me to show you poetry in motion and I will show you a horse. ~ Unknown

Day 115: All you need for happiness is a good run, a good horse, and a good wife. ~ Daniel Boone

Day 116: Your horse can only be as brave as you are. ~ Unknown

Day 117: Riding a horse is not a gentle hobby, to be picked up and laid down like a game of Solitaire. It's a grand passion. ~ Ralph Waldo Emerson

Day 118: A stubborn horse walks behind you, an impatient horse walks in front of you, but a noble companion walks beside you. ~ Unknown

Day 119: Through the days of celebration and joy, and the dark days of mourning—the faithful horse has always been with us. ~ Unknown

Day 120: The horse stares at its captor, barely remembering the free kicks of youth. ~ Mason Cooley

Day 121: There is just as much horse sense as ever, but the horses have most of it. ~ Unknown

Day 122: Whoever said a horse was dumb, was dumb. ~ Unknown Cowboy Saying

Day 123: My horses are my friends not my slaves. ~ Unknown

Day 124: I can make a General in five minutes but a good horse is hard to replace. ~ Abraham Lincoln

Day 125:I'd call him a sadistic, hippophilic necrophile, but that would be beating a dead horse. ~ Woody Allen

Day 126: Horses change lives. They give our young people confidence and self esteem. They provide peace and tranquility to troubled souls—they give us hope! ~ Unknown

Day 127: It is not enough for a man to know how to ride. He must know how to fall. ~ Mexican Proverb

Day 128: If your horse says no, you either asked the wrong question, or asked the question wrong. ~ Unknown

Day 129: A true horse person is someone who not just loves to ride, but LIVES to ride. Friends leave when life is boring and boyfriends leave when life is tough, but a horse will always be with you. ~ Unknown

Day 130: We ought to do good to others as simply as a horse runs, or a bee makes honey, or a vine bears grapes, season after season without thinking of the grapes it has borne. ~ Marcus Aurelius

Day 131: Tell me it can't be done, and I will do it. Tell me the goal is too high, and I will reach it. Place an obstacle in front of me and I will soar over it. Challenge me, dare me, or even defy me, or even defy me. But do NOT underestimate me. For on the back of my horse, anything is possible. ~ Unknown

Day 132: Some people say riding isn't a sport, but I'd love to see them try. ~ Unknown

Day 133: Home is where the horse is…So I'll be in the barn. ~ Unknown

Day 134: If you want to know about a horse's life, just look into his eyes. ~ Unknown

Day 135: It is best we should not all think alike; it is a difference of opinion that makes horse races. ~ Mark Twain

Day 136: The worst part of riding is when you have to dismount. ~ Unknown

Day 137: In life, horses are some of the best friends you'll ever have! ~ Unknown

Day 138: Horses are proof God loves us. ~ Unknown

Day 139: Heaven is on the back of a horse. ~ Unknown

Day 140: Alimony is like buying hay for a dead horse. ~ Groucho Marx

Day 141: When I fall off my horse, I don't check and make sure I'm alright, I'll be just fine. I check the horse and make sure he is alright. ~ Unknown

Day 142: Horses are different than people. They never stop loving. ~ Unknown

Day 143: If you live a life without horses, you don't have a life at all. ~ Unknown

Day 144: You can take a horse out of the wild, but you can't take the wild out of the horse. ~ Unknown

Day 145: Flaming enthusiasm, backed up by horse sense and persistence, is the quality that most frequently makes for success. ~ Dale Carnegie

Day 146: A barn isn't a barn if there are no horses in it. ~ Unknown

Day 147: In the quiet light of the stable, you hear a muffled snort, a stamp of the hoof, a friendly nicker. Gentle eyes inquire, "How are you my old friend?" and suddenly all your troubles fade away. ~ Unknown

Day 148: My horse teaches me everything I need to know about myself. ~ Unknown

Day 149: Strength lies within the heart, but the strength to trust lies between the horse and his rider. ~ Unknown

Day 150: Nothing is more sacred as the bond between a horse and rider. No other creature can become so emotionally close to a human as a horse. When a horse dies, the memory lives on, because an enormous part of his owner's heart, soul, and very existence dies also. ~ Stephanie M. Thorn

Day 151: What's scarier when mad? A two hundred pound football player or a twelve hundred pound mare? Riding is a real sport with real athletes. If horseback riding was easy they would call it football. ~ Unknown

Day 152: You know you are a eal horse person when you start clucking at people to move. ~ Unknown

Day 153: The only real place for a true horse lover is on the back of a horse. ~ Unknown

Day 154: You fell off your horse and you cried. I fell off my horse and I got back on. ~ Unknown

Day 155: Nothing moves me more than on the way to fetching in my mare in the morning—than the sound of her neighing to me as I open the gate. ~ Unknown

Day 156: It's true all right. Hours spent in the barn are life's stolen pleasures. ~ Unknown

Day 157: Seven days without a horse, makes one weak. ~ Unknown

Day 158: No philosophers so thoroughly understand us as dogs and horses. ~ Herman Melville

Day 159: Every time I count my blessings, I count my horse twice. ~ Unknown

Day 160: Our perfect companions never have less than four feet. ~ Unknown

Day 161: If I smell like peppermints, I was giving my horse a treat. If I smell like shampoo, I was giving my horse a bath. If I smell like manure, I tripped. ~ Unknown

Day 162: A world without horses is like a heart without a beat. ~ Unknown

Day 163: Anyone who says a horse doesn't understand what you say never tried talking to one. ~ Unknown

Day 164: A life without horses is possible, but pointless. ~ Unknown

Day 165: People on the back of horses look better than they are. People in cars look worse than they are. ~ Marya Mannes

Day 166: I am not a Cowgirl. I am a Horsegirl. ~ Unknown

Day 167: If you think I'm quiet, it's only because we're not talking about horses. ~ Unknown

Day 168: Thunder is the sound of hoof beats in heaven. ~ Unknown

Day 169: Never ride faster than your guardian angel can fly. ~ Unknown

Day 170: Riding isn't the matter of life or death. It's more important than that. ~ Unknown

Day 171: A horse is dangerous at both ends and uncomfortable in the middle. ~ Ian Fleming

Day 172: You don't think a horse can count? Put three carrots in your pocket and give your horse only two. ~ Unknown

Day 173: A horse is not your partner until you learn to listen to him. ~ Unknown

Day 174: I was a normal girl and then I started horse riding. ~ Unknown

Day 175: Some of my best leading men have been dogs and horses. ~ Elizabeth Taylor

Day 176: Man's best friend may be his dog, but a woman's best friend is her horse. ~ Unknown

Day 177: Great riders are not great because of their talent, they are great because of their passion. ~ Unknown

Day 178: Horses are like potato chips. You can never have just one. ~ Unknown

Day 179: If it has nothing to do with horses, count me out. ~ Unknown

Day 180: The history of mankind is carried on the back of the horse. ~ Unknown

Day 181: A rider without a horse is just a human, but a horse without a rider is still a horse. ~ Unknown

Day 182: For anyone who doesn't like horses, freedom and life means nothing to you. ~ Unknown

Day 183: You can say whatever you like bad about me, but don't speak badly about my horses. ~ Unknown

Day 184: I'd rather be dumped by a horse than a man. ~ Unknown

Day 185: The joy of horses is not the riding, jumping, racing, showing, or grooming, but of owning. ~ Unknown

Day 186: With horses there is no favorite. ~ Unknown

Day 187: You don't truly trust a horse until you can forget the saddle. ~ Unknown

Day 188: A girl's gotta believe something. I believe I'll go riding. ~ Unknown

Day 189: Horses are God's apology for men. ~ Unknown

Day 190: The more I meet men, the better my horse looks. ~ Unknown

Day 191: The hardest thing about riding is the ground. ~ Unknown

Day 192: Treat him well, for he has a loyal heart and soul and is willing to risk his life for his rider and companion. ~ Unknown

Day 193: You can have my boyfriend, but stay away from my horse. ~ Unknown

Day 194: Born to ride—forced to work. ~ Unknown

Day 195: The world is best viewed through the ears of a horse. ~ Unknown

Day 196: I never had a real friend until I started riding. ~ Unknown

Day 197: A perfect day for me, without horses? Neigh I don't think so. ~ Unknown

Day 198: Don't flatter yourself cowboy, I was just looking at your horse. ~ Unknown

Day 199: Eat, Sleep, Ride. ~ Unknown

Day 200: There comes a point in every rider's life when he wonders if it's all worth it. Then one look at his horse and he realizes—it is. ~ Kelly Stewart

Day 201: My barrel horse is smarter than your honor student. ~ Unknown

Day 202: When people say I'm obsessed with horses, it's an understatement. ~ Unknown

Day 203: Yes, I smell like horses. Your point is?? ~ Unknown

Day 204: He who said he made a small fortune in the horse business probably started out with s large fortune. ~ Unknown

Day 205: There is nothing like a rattling ride for curing melancholy. ~ Pared

Day 206: If you don't love your horse at his worst, then you don't deserve him at his best. ~ Unknown

Day 207: Never been a horse that can't be Rode. Never been a Cowboy that can't be thrown. ~ Unknown

Day 208: As distance shows a horse's strength, so time reveals a person's heart. ~ Chinese Proverb

Day 209: I heard a neigh, Oh, such a brisk and melodious neigh it was. My heart leaped with the sound. ~ Nathaniel Hawthorne

Day 210: Throw your heart over a fence and your horse will follow. ~ Unknown

Day 211: The last time somebody pointed out that cowboys ride horses, not tricycles, I shot him. Of course I waited until another gunslinger gunned him down, but nevertheless I still shot him. ~ Jarod Kintz

Day 212: We rode the merry go round like a couple of lovers. We weren't though; we were just two horse enthusiasts from two different worlds. (I think she was from Mars.) ~ Jarod Kintz

Day 213: In riding horses, we borrow freedom. ~ Helen Thompson

Day 214: A man on a horse is spiritually as well as physically bigger than a man on foot. ~ John Steinbeck

Day 215: To understand the soul of a horse is the closest we humans can come to knowing perfection. ~ Unknown

Day 216: There is a lot of folklore about equestrian statues, especially the ones with riders on them. There is said to be a code in the number and placement of the horse's hooves: If one of the horse's hooves is in the air, the rider was wounded in battle; two legs in the air means that the rider was killed in battle; three legs in the air indicates that the rider got lost on the way to the battle; and four legs in the air means that the sculptor was very, very clever. Five legs in the air means that there's probably at least one other horse standing behind the horse you're looking at; and the rider lying on the ground with his horse lying on top of him with all four legs in the air means that the rider was either a very incompetent horseman or owned a very bad-tempered horse. ~ Terry Pratchett

Day 217: When I bestride him, I soar, I am a hawk: he trots the air; the earth sings when he touches it; the basest horn of his hoof is more musical than the pipe of Hermes. ~ William Shakespeare

Day 218: When I hear somebody talk about a horse or cow being stupid; I figure it's a sure sign that the animal has somehow outfoxed them. ~ Tom Dorrance

Day 219: I've spent most my life riding horses. The rest I've just wasted. ~ Anonymous

Day 220: When God wanted to create a horse, he said to the South Wind, "I want to make a creature of you. Condense." And the wind condensed. ~ Amir Abd-el-Kader

Day 221: Employers are like horses—they require management. ~ P.G. Wodehouse

Day 222: "I don't like people," said Velvet. "... I only like horses." ~ Enid Bagnold

Day 223: You can lead a horse to water, but you can't make him participate in synchronized diving. ~ Cuthbert Soup

Day 224: A horse gallops with its lungs, perseveres with its heart and wins with its character. ~ Tessio

Day 225: To ride or not to ride—this is a stupid question. ~ Bandy Michelle

Day 226: A horse which stops dead just before a jump and thus propels its rider into a graceful arc provides a splendid excuse for general merriment. ~ H.R.H. Prince Philip

Day 227: A horse loves freedom, and the weariest old work horse will roll on the ground or break into a lumbering gallop when he is turned loose into the open. ~ Gerald Raftery

Day 228: But what truly horsey girls discover in the end is that boyfriends, husbands, children, and careers are the substitute-for horses. ~ Jane Smiley

Day 229: Those who get in the way of love's path will be kicked by horses. ~ Bisco Hatori

Day 230: When riding a horse, we leave our fear, troubles, and sadness behind on the ground. ~ Juli Carlson

Day 231: "Let me drive," she said, reaching for the reins. He turned to her in disbelief. "This is a phaeton, not a single-horse wagon."
Sophie fought the urge to throttle him. His nose was running, his eyes were red, he couldn't stop coughing, and still he found the energy to act like an arrogant peacock. "I assure you," she said slowly, "that I know how to drive a team of horses." ~ Julia Quinn

Day 232: Horses were never wrong. They always did what they did for a reason, and it was up to you to figure it out. ~ Jeannette Walls

Day 233: I may not be a horse whisperer, but I certainly can and do shout at unicorns. ~ Jarod Kintz

Day 234: Don't be the rider who gallops all night and never sees the horse beneath him. ~ Jelaluddin Rumi

Day 235: When riding my horse, I no longer have my heart in my chest but between my knees. ~ Unknown

Day 236: There are Navajo teachings about how a car works. This vehicle is very much like a horse, operating on the same principles. The automobile is considered more "intelligent," and we think of it in such terms. The automobile is mad eof iron and steel taken from the earth. This iron is the earth's spirit, which has been made into the body of the automobile. The trees, as vegetation, were also taken from the earth and made into rubber for the tires. The air, or spirit, is the same as that of a horse's breath of life, instilled in its body. The arms and legs of the auto makes it move. Then there are the dark storm clouds and heavenly bodies like lightning, which are found inside the auto to give it power. This is exactly the same power the horse has.

Water, which comes from the earth, is put into the auto for its cooling system. Oil from the earth is similar to the fat from the earth a horse receives. Just as gasoline comes from the earth as fuel, plants are in a horse's body to make it operate. Therefore, horses and cars are the same in every way. ~ John Holiday

Day 237: I used to have straw-colored hair. Horses loved it ~ Jarod Kintz

Day 238: She let them go all night and in the mornings would find them coming toward her where she slept, with that alert and nervous air unridden horses always have at dawn. They are remembering some far time when predators came for them at first light. So they came toward her with the strange and painful air of fallen angels, treading carefully and slowly as if the earth were foreign soil. ~ Paulette Jiles

Day 239: Sell the cow, buy the sheep, but never be without the horse. ~ Irish Proverb

Day 240: When you are on a great horse, you have the best seat you will ever have. ~ Sir Winston Churchill

Day 241: I am fond of the sound of horses in the night. The lifting of feet. Stamping. The clicking of their iron shoes against rock. They mouth one anothers withers and rear and squeal and whirl and shuffle and cough and stand and snort. There is the combined rumblings of each individual gut. They sound larger than they are. The air tastes of horses, ripples as though come alive with their good-hearted strength and stamina. ~ Mark Spragg

Day 242: There is no happiness like the pounding of so many horses into one. I imagine I hear the horses laugh. I think it every time. I think that running is the way a horse may laugh out loud. When I am older I will believe that following in their wake has filled me with the inconsolable joy of animals. ~ Mark Spragg

Day 243: Oats. A grain, which in England is generally given to horses, but in Scotland supports the people. ~ Samuel Johnson

Day 244: There is no secret so close as that between a rider and his horse. ~ Robert Smith Surtees

Day 245: When your horse follows you without being asked, when he rubs your head on yours, and when you look at him and feel a tingle down your spine, you know you are loved. Do you love him back? ~ Unknown

Day 246: Harriet was silent. She suddenly saw Wimsey in a new light. She knew him to be intelligent, clean, courteous, wealthy, well-read, amusing and enamoured, but he had not so far produced in her that crushing sense of utter inferiority which leads to prostration and hero-worship. But she now realised that there was, after all, something god-like about him. He could control a horse. ~ Dorothy L. Sayers

Day 247: When gangs took over the [abandoned public land in Philadelphia] and the neighborhood took a turn for the worse, horses became a way of saving lives. By getting boys interested in raising a horse rather than killing another human being, these cowboys gave the youth something positive: father figures, focus, and the ability to stand tall. ~ G. Neri, Ghetto Cowboy

Day 248: Before I sold used cars, I sold used horses. Mostly to glue factories. ~ Jarod Kintz

Day 249: He doth nothing but talk of his horses. ~ William Shakespeare

Day 250: "You can lead a horse to water but you can't make it drink," is an old saying that is not exactly true, because anybody that's ever been around horses would know if the horse didn't want to go to the water, it wouldn't. ~ Unknown

Day 251: As my mom used to say, "If wishes were horses, we'd be up to our eyeballs in shit. ~ Cat Adams

Day 252: It's a lot like nuts and bolts. If the rider's nuts, the horse bolts. ~ Nicholas Evans

Day 253: Did you ever see an unhappy horse? Did you ever see a horse that had the blues? One reason why birds and horses are not unhappy is because they are not trying to impress other birds and horses. ~ Dale Carnegie

Day 254: The wagon rests in winter, the sleigh in summer, and the horse never. ~ Yiddish Proverb

Day 255: Whoever said money couldn't buy happiness didn't know where to buy a horse.

Day 256: Horses, and children, I often think, have a lot of good sense in the world. ~ Josephine Demott Robinson

Day 257: A horseman should know neither fear nor anger. ~ Unknown

Day 258: Experienced riders are not prone to brag. And usually newcomers, if they start out being boastful, end up being modest. ~ Unknown

Day 259: If the world were truly a rational place, men would ride sidesaddle. ~ Rita Mae Brown

Day 260: Who among us as a child has not asked Santa to bring us a pony on Christmas day? ~ Unknown

Day 261: The hardest thing about learning to ride is the ground. ~ Unknown

Day 262: When your horse follows you without being asked, when he rubs his head on yours, and when you look at him and feel a tingle down your spine...you know you are loved. ~ John Lyons

Day 263: It is the difficult horses that have the most to give you. ~ Lendon Gray

Day 264: It is not enough for a man to know how to ride; he must know how to fall. ~ Mexican Proverb

Day 265: You cannot train a horse with shouts and expect it to obey a whisper. ~ Dagobert Runes

Day 266: Wherever man has left his footprint from the long ascent from barbarism to civilization we will find the hoof print of a horse beside it. ~ John Trotwood Moore

Day 267: Stay away from a horse long enough and you'll start tapping your fingers to the beat of a trot. ~ Unknown

Day 268: The horse, the noblest, bravest, proudest, most courageous, and certainly the most perverse and infuriating animal that humans ever domesticated. ~ Anne McCaffrey

Day 269: In buying a horse or taking a wife, shut your eyes tight and commend yourself to God. ~ Tuscan Proverb

Day 270: If God had intended man to walk, he would have given him four legs. Instead, he gave him two—one to put n either side of a horse. ~ Unknown

Day 271: They say princes learn no art truly, but the art of horsemanship. The reason is, the brave beast is no flatterer.

He will throw a prince as soon as his groom. ~ Ben Johnson

Day 272: Many people have sighed for the 'good old days' and regretted the 'passing of the horse.' But today, when only those who like horses own them, it is a far better time for horses. ~ C.W. Anderson

Day 273: Horses have hooves to carry them over frost and snow; hair to protect them from wind and cold. They eat grass and drink water, and fling up their heels...Such is the nature of the horse. ~ Chang Tzu

Day 274: My dear, I don't care what they do, so long as they don't do it in the streets and frighten the horses. ~ Mrs. Patrick Campbell

Day 275: I have seen things so beautiful, that they have brought tears to my eyes. Yet, none of them match the gracefulness and the beauty of a horse running free. ~ Unknown

Day 276: The horse, the horse! The symbol of surging potency and power of movement, of action. ~ D.H. Lawrence

Day 277: In dealing with a girl or a horse, one lets nature take its course. ~ Fred Astaire

Day 278: The horse has such a docile nature that he would always rather do right than wrong, if he can only be taught to distinguish one from the other. ~ George Melville

Day 279: As a horse runs, think of it as a game of tag with the wind. ~ Tre Tuberville

Day 280: I live in a house, but my home is in a stable. ~ Unknown

Day 281: A horse is a horse, of course, of course. ~ Jay Livingston and Ray Evans

Day 282: Old minds are like horses; you must exercise them if you wish to keep them in working order. ~ John Adams

Day 283: I'd rather have a goddamned horse. A horse is at least human for God's sake. ~ J.D. Salinger

Day 284: When God created the horse, he said to the magnificent creature: I have made thee as no other. All the treasure of the earth shall lie between the lies. Thou shalt cast they enemies between thy hooves, but thou shalt carry my friends upon thy back. Thy saddle shall be the seat of prayers to me. And thou fly without any wings, and conquer without any sword. ~ The Koran

Day 285: I have often been asked why I like horses so much. Look into one's eyes. There you will see generations of horses who have served the humans for thousands of years for nothing in return. Beaten horses, starved horses, horses who no longer possess a spirit. They deserve to be loved and respected as much as humanly possible. Let them run free again. Let them no longer be a faithful beast, but embrace them as you would a dear friend, for that is what they are. ~ Unknown

Day 286: My horses understand me tolerably well. I converse with them at least four hours every day. They are strangers to the bridle and saddle; they live in great amity with me, and friendship to each other. ~ Jonathan Swift

Day 287: Horses are predictably unpredictable. ~ Loretta Grace

Day 288: Whether you regard the horse with aw or love, it is impossible to escape the sheer power of his presence. ~ Mary Wanless

Day 289: When you're young and fall off your horse, you may break something. When you're my age and you fall off, you splatter. ~ Roy Rogers

Day 290: How to ride a horse:
Step One—Mount the horse.
Step Two—Stay mounted.

Day 291: No ride is ever the last. No horse is ever the last one you will have. Somehow there will be other horses, other places to ride them. ~ Monica Dickens

Day 292: Dog lovers hate to clean out their kennels. Horse lovers like cleaning out their stables. ~ Monica Dickens

Day 293: When I can't ride anymore, I shall keep horses as long as I can hobble about with a bucket and a wheelbarrow. When I can't hobble, I shall roll my wheelchair out to the field where my horses graze and watch them. ~ Monica Dickens

Day 294: If one induces the horse to assume that carriage which it would adopt of its own accord when displaying beauty, then, one directs the horse to appear joyous and magnificent, proud and remarkable for having been ridden. ~ Xenophen

Day 295: How do you catch a loose horse? Make a noise like a carrot. ~ British Calvary joke

Day 296: They're the most forgiving creatures God ever made. ~ Nicholas Evans

Day 297: The horses paw and prance and neigh, fillies and colts like kittens play, and dance and toss their rippled manes, shining and soft as silken skeins. ~ Oliver Wendell Holmes

Day 298: Be wary of the horse with a sense of humor. ~ Pam Brown

Day 299: A horse! A horse! My kingdom for a horse! ~ William Shakespeare

Day 300: Horses give us the wings we lack. ~ Unknown

Day 301: What we are seeking so frantically elsewhere may turn out to be the horse we have been riding all along. ~ Harvey Cox

Day 302: A camel is a horse designed by committee. ~ Alec Issigonis

Day 303: In westerns you were permitted to kiss your horse but never your girl. ~ Gary Cooper

Day 304: Horses are so forgiving. ~ Tom Dorrance

Day 305: Horses can't talk, but they can speak if you listen. ~ Unknown

Day 306: That some people are happy to live their life around horses is almost as baffling as the fact that horses are happy to live their life around humans. ~ Unknown

Day 307: The sight of that horse did something to me I've never been able to explain. He was more than tremendous strength and speed and beauty of motion. He set me dreaming. ~ Walt Morey

Day 308: Yet when the books have been read, it boils down to the horse, his human companion, and what goes on between them. ~ Walter Farley

Day 309: Trust in God but tie your horse. ~ Unknown

Day 310: Horses are the dolphins of the plains, the spirits of the wind; yet we sit astride them for the sake of being well-groomed, whereas they could have all the desire in the world to bolt, but instead, they adjust their speed and grace only to please us, never to displease. ~ Lauren Salerno

Day 311: To me, horses and freedom are synonymous. ~ Veryl Goodnight

Day 312: Horses have never hurt anyone yet, except when they bet on them. ~ Stuarte Cloete

Day 313: I go about looking at horses and cattle. They eat grass, make love, work when they have to, bear their young. I am sick with envy of them. ~ Sherwood Anderson

Day 314: Speak to your mind but ride a fast horse. ~ Unknown

Day 315: Horseback riding is life, the rest is just details. ~ Unknown

Day 316: Boot, saddle to horse, and away. ~ Robert Browning

Day 317: Four things greater than all things are—Women and Horses and Power and War. ~ Rudyard Kipling

Day 318: Other animals ran only when they had a reason, but the horse would run for no reason whatever, as if to run out of his own skin. ~ Rabindranath Tagore

Day 319: Honor lies in the mane of a horse. ~ Herman Melville

Day 320: Horse sense is a thing a horse has, which keeps it from betting on people. ~ W.C. Fields

Day 321: We shall take great care not to annoy the horse and spoil his friendly charm, for it is like the scent of a blossom—once lost it will never return. ~ Pluvinel

Day 322: Whether you regard the horse with awe or love, it is impossible to escape the sheer power of his presence. ~ Mary Wanless

Day 323: A good man will take care of his horses and dogs. Not only when they are young, but also when they are old and past service. ~ Plutarch

Day 324: A pony is a childhood dream, a horse is an adulthood treasure. ~Rebecca Carrol

Day 325: Horse…if God made anything more beautiful, he kept it for himself. ~ Unknown

Day 326: For the sake of argument and illustration I will presume that certain articles of ordinary diet, however beneficial in youth, are prejudicial in advanced life, like beans to a horse, whose common ordinary food is hay and corn. ~ William Banting

Day 327: I'd like to play a horse, many people think I already have. Either end of the horse would be fine. ~ Dawn French

Day 328: If a poet knows more about a horse than he does about heaven, he might better stick to a horse, and someday the horse may carry him into heaven. ~ Charles Ives

Day 329: And God took a handful of southerly wind, blew his breath upon it, and created the horse. ~ Bedouin legend

Day 330: He knows when you are happy. He knows when you are proud. He also knows when you have a carrot. ~ Unknown

Day 331: I ended the war a horse ahead. ~ Nathan Bedford Forrest

Day 332: I'm named after a horse. My mom's best friend had a horse named Brooke, so my Dad suggested Brooklyn as a more formal version, and it just stuck—and now I live in Brooklyn part-time so go figure. ~ Brooklyn Decker

Day 333: Without knowing this, no man can dress a horse perfectly. ~ William Cavendish

Day 334: Horse, thou art truly a creature without equal, for thou flyest without wings, and conquerest without sword. ~ The Koran

Day 335: Give me food and drink and care for me. And when the day's work is done, shelter me. Give me a clean bed and leave me not a too small place in the stable. Talk to me, for your voice often takes the place of the reins. Be good to me and I shall serve you more gladly and love you.

Day 336: But my method of the pillar, as it throws the horse yet more upon the haunches, is still more effectual to this purpose, and besides always gives him the ply to the side he goes of. ~ William Cavendish

Day 337: The horse's neck is between the two reigns of the bridle, which both meet in the rider's hand. ~ William Cavendish

Day 338: And he said that a horse was not dressed, whose curb was not loose, said right; and it is equally true that the curb can never play, when in its right place, except the horse be upon his haunches. ~ William Cavendish

Day 339: I can always tell which is the front of the horse, but beyond that, my art is not above the ordinary. ~ Mark Twain

Day 340: Give a horse what he needs and he will give you his heart in return. ~ Unknown

Day 341: But there is nothing to be done till a horse's head is settled. ~ William Cavendish

Day 342: But we ought to consider the natural form and shape of a horse, that we may work him according to nature. ~ William Cavendish

Day 343: Yes it's true I once knocked out a horse. It was at a fiesta in my mother's home of Guarare. Someone bet me a bottle of whiskey that I couldn't do it. ~ Roberto Duran

Day 344: O for a horse with wings. ~ William Shakespeare

Day 345: Feeling down? Saddle up. It's the only cure. ~ Unknown

Day 346: As a young girl, I think I wanted to be a horse woman. I loved horses. ~ Karen Hughes

Day 347: Being born in a stable does not make one a horse. ~ Arthur Wellesley

Day 348: You never know how a horse will pull until you hook him to a heavy load. ~ Paul Bryant

Day 349: The horse is God's gift to mankind. ~ Arabian Saying

Day 350: Closeness, friendship, affection—keeping your own horse means all of these things. ~ Bertrand Leclair

Day 351: The word chivalry is derived from the French cheval, the horse. ~ Thomas Bulfinch

Day 352: You're better off betting on a horse than betting on a man. A horse may not be able to hold you tight, but he doesn't wanna wander from the stable at night. ~ Betty Grable

Day 353: If a man carries his horse out of a slave state into a free one, he does not lose his property interest in him; but if he carries his slave into a free state, the law makes him free. ~ Benjamin F. Wade

Day 354: God forbid that I should go to heaven where there are no horses. ~ R.B. Cunningham-Graham

Day 355: Bread may feed my body, but my horse feeds my soul. ~ Unknown

Day 356: In our sport you are lucky to find a horse of a lifetime and I found mine relatively early. He's done everything for me and I owe him the world. ~ Zara Phillips

Day 357: When a man's mind rides faster than his horse can gallop they quickly both tire. ~ John Webster

Day 358: So I see technology as a Trojan horse: It looks like a wonderful thing, but they are going to regret introducing it into the schools because it simply can't be controlled. ~ Daniel Greenberg

Day 359: In riding a horse, we borrow freedom. ~ Helen Thompson

Day 360: Arabians are a little bit of everything perfect. ~ Amanda Ferber

Day 361: It's been argued that of all the animals humans have domesticated, the horse is the most important to our history. For thousands of years, horses were our most reliable transportation. ~ Elton Gallegly

Day 362: I was like a race horse, just trying to get into the world. ~ Joey Fischer

Day 363: Industry is a better horse to ride than genius. ~ Walter Lippman

Day 364: If you act like you've only got fifteen minutes, it'll take all day. Act like you've got all day and it'll take fifteen minutes. ~ Monty Roberts

Day 365: A racehorse is a creature that can take several thousand people for a ride at the same time. ~ Unknown

**Collect the entire series
365 Days of Happiness
inspirational quote books**

365 Days of Romance
365 Days of America
365 Days of the Bible
365 Days of Cats
365 Days of Dogs
365 Days of Horses

17300993R00029

Made in the USA
San Bernardino, CA
08 December 2014